HOW TO LAUNCH A MAGAZINE FOR PROFESSIONAL PUBLISHERS

BUSINESS FOR BREAKFAST VOLUME EIGHT

BLAZE WARD

How to Launch a Magazine for Professional Publishers
Business for Breakfast, Volume 8
Copyright © 2018 Blaze Ward
All rights reserved
Published 2018 by Knotted Road Press
www.KnottedRoadPress.com

ISBN: 978-1-943663-84-2

Disclaimer

Never miss a release!

If you'd like to be notified of new releases, sign up for my newsletter.

I only send out newsletters once a quarter, will never spam you, or use your email for nefarious purposes. You can also unsubscribe at any time.
http://www.BlazeWard.com/newsletter/

AUTHOR'S NOTE

I'm being blackmailed to write this, so you people better appreciate my efforts.

And when you see YMMV, apparently there are some folks that have never heard the phrase "Your Mileage May Vary." Learn it. Live it. Understand it.

BW
West of the Mountains, WA
20180712

THIS IS BOUNDARY SHOCK QUARTERLY'S STORY...

The document you are holding is the culmination of my desire to create my own quarterly speculative fiction magazine, at the point where the seventh revolution in Indie Publishing suddenly put the necessary tools in my hands. I don't have to rely on kickstarting, or a major publishing house, or a lot of debt.

Over the last year, I was able to put together a document of intent, recruit a Syndicate of writers to contribute stories, and eventually start publishing the magazine. The costs are remarkably low, if you work at it, and are willing to invest in the few necessary, time-saving tools that I will talk about deeper in this book.

So what did I do?

Quarterly

Speculative Fiction (science fiction with a more intellectual intent, which is not the same as execution)

Indie

Magazine

This Business For Breakfast book: *How to Launch a Magazine for Professional Publishers* is intended to guide you through the process I followed to get there, with the expectation that many of you will choose to follow in my footsteps and create your own magazines in the future. The tools are only going to get easier, over time, so you can do it.

What you need is will and organization. An investment in some of the tools I will talk about, which will pay off quickly in time saved.

And desire.

So let's get started.

BUNDLE RABBIT & COLLABORATION: A BACKGROUND

Bundles

One of the more interesting tools for writers these days is what we call Bundles. There are several companies that do bundles, but there are interesting rules you need to be aware of.

First, most bundles run on the artificial scarcity model. What that means is that the bundle is usually only available for a very limited time. Three weeks is a normal run, and then the bundle will be gone forever. This plays on your need to get it immediately.

The second frequent characteristic of bundles is tiers. For something like $10 US, you get *these* five novels, but if you increase your contribution to $20US, you can get the whole set (normally 10 novels or novel-length titles and collections).

Frequently, bundles are also limited to novels (or novel-sized collections), and are limited to ten books. Useful, but rigid and unforgiving, especially if you write a number of novellas, like I do.

Another thing to take into account is that the folks invited to be in bundles tend to already be big names (or at least big enough) or they have to know somebody. As of the beginning of 2018, as I write this, so-called Traditional Publishing (the New York folks) have been ending their relationships with many authors for a while, and it has reached the point where former major best-selling authors are being offered greatly reduced contracts, if they can get a contract at all.

Frequently, they are getting the rights back to their own books and are starting to publish them in the indie space.

For a new writer trying to break out and get some coverage, it can be nearly impossible to get into a major bundle unless you know someone, or have written the perfect novel for a very weird theme. (Or have a reputation that you could be asked to step in and write something on an impossible deadline and make it. Did that, once.)

So while bundles are a good deal for the folks who can get into them, the major players are not accessible to the rest of us. That's where Bundle Rabbit comes in.

Bundle Rabbit

The Bundle Rabbit project (www.bundlerabbit.com) was something that a friend of mine who is a software developer put together. He wanted to create a tool for Indie writers to build their own bundles (the Do-It-Yourself model). Many new authors don't have the tools to market themselves widely and gain exposure, especially not if they are writing shorter fiction than novels.

In a bundle, a curator comes up with a concept, then builds a project by locating stories in the marketplace that fit their theme or by reaching out to people and asking if they have something that fits. They can include stories of any length, from flash fiction all the way up to novels, and any combination therein. This works in favor of newer authors, who tend to work on short fiction to hone their craft, before going out and trying to write an epic fantasy series in ten books.

Also breaking the bundle model above, bundles can run forever, if everyone agrees. I've had bundles still making sales a year later, because I had a new fan, or someone else had a new fan, who grabbed the bundle when they discovered one of us.

The work of marketing a bundle falls onto the authors themselves, rather than the bundling website, but it gives each author in the bundle the chance to reach all the fans of all the other writers who participate. This is a collective marketing gig, as much as anything.

Generally, you aren't going to get rich on any one bundle. That's not the point of doing this. You are getting exposure, because people wanting to read on a theme might find you. Or if the bundle is new work, then fans of each of the writers will want to buy it and maybe read the rest of the stories. In terms of unit sales, Bundle Rabbit is currently my number two distributor. In terms of money, it is much closer to the bottom. But this is about exposure.

And Discoverability for the new writer trying to reach readers.

The technical side, the so-called secret sauce, is that Bundle Rabbit (Kydala Press) handles the effort to push the bundle out to the various distributors (Amazon, iTunes, etc.), so the writers don't have to. Bundle Rabbit will also handle all the money that comes in. Usually, the biggest single obstacle to any kind of collective marketing project is how to divide up the money as well as how to make sure each authors gets paid correctly and on time.

The downside to bundling is that each author who wants to play has to upload their story individually. This means designing and building a professional-looking cover, writing marketing copy for the blurb, and then making it available in the Bundle Rabbit marketplace. This can be a daunting task for new writers.

So the good folks at the Bundle Rabbit came up with Collaboration.

Phase Two: Collaboration

Unlike bundling, the collaborative project allows much more control and flexibility. Each author sends their story manuscript to the central editor without having to deal with cover and marketing issues. In that way, a collaboration project is more like a pure, traditionally-published anthology.

The editor then puts together the project, loads a single cover for all of it, and writes the back cover marketing materials.

As before, once the project is completed, Bundle Rabbit handles the task of pushing the electronic and print books out to the various distributor, saving a lot of effort on the part of the editor. Also, money is handled directly by Bundle Rabbit, and sent directly to the authors regularly, so the editor is not on the hook to track the money or exercise any fiduciary responsibilities.

One important place where a collaboration is different from a bundle is that the editor running the project can set different payment ratios for all the authors (and possibly artists) involved.

Perhaps one author is a big name, and negotiated a bigger slice of the pie. In any case, once the rates are set, each author gets paid on that ratio as long as the book is available.

As with other bundles done on Bundle Rabbit, they can stay up forever earning nickels. ("Them nickels spend.") People can come along later and find them.

There is still a lot of work for the editor, but for the authors, they just have to write the best story they can and send it in. As an editor, I'm going to take a share for my publishing house, separate from the share I get as a writer in this issue. Similarly, you can put your cover artist in for a share, instead of paying them up front.

Phase Three: Mindset

Doing a Collaborative project is a different mindset from handling things the old way. Traditional magazines accepted a story, and then paid on publication, and the author was done. In the way old days (1960, for example), the major SF mags paid generally around 1-2 cents a word for the average authors, so an author who could place a story every few months could have a very comfortable, middle-class lifestyle as a result. Much more recently, they are paying six and sometimes ten cents a word, but inflation in the last sixty years has been such that you can't make a living on just short fiction. The math won't work and you'll need a day job.

With the rise of the internet, new tools for funding a magazine have become available, and folks have begun using them. One of the most prominent right now is to crowd-fund your anthology project, using websites like Kickstart or Indigogo. You put up a project pitch, advertise the hell out of it, and try to get folks to subscribe. If it works, you might manage to get the $5,000 US you need to put out a professional-looking anthology, with good cover art, paying professional rates to your authors, and still make a little money on the side as the editor, with the hope that long-term, you earn enough to make it worth your while.

Not all of them work out, so you might have a great idea, but not meet the funding threshold. You could, I suppose, run up the costs on your credit card. I would not recommend that.

Some small and medium-sized publishers try to make a go of it by doing a modified royalty-share model, where they will get all the money that comes in initially, and then begin paying authors on a per-share model, once the project has earned out the advance costs. If they can make that work, more power to them. I have been in situations where I have never earned a single penny.

All that brings us back around the Bundle Rabbit Collaboration. This was always a royalty-share project. As an editor, I put in the sweat equity: organizing the project, paying for the art and the cover designer, doing any editing, etc. In return, I get a share of the money that comes in, but only a share. If we make a sale for our first dollar, then I might get a quarter, and everyone else splits the remaining seventy-five cents. But I only get paid when you do. You only get paid if the project does well.

It is INCUMBENT on the participating authors to hype the project. You have to tell all your fans so they come buy it. Tell complete strangers in a coffee shop. Tell the woman next to you on the train. Whatever it takes, because that's the only way a project like this works.

In trade, if every author involved brings in all their fans, they gain access to everyone else's fans at the same time. I like reading Author A, and discover Author B and Author J along the way, so I go buy their books, too.

Money. It's all about the money.

3

WHERE I WENT

I have wanted to do my own science fiction magazine as an ongoing project, rather than a one-shot anthology, for a very long time. When I learned about Bundle Rabbit's new capabilities, I sat down and tried to figure out how to make it work.

Traditionally-published anthologies and magazines require a huge upfront investment, paying all of the authors and editors long before the publisher ever sees a penny of return, with no promise of ever breaking even. So not going there.

You can try crowd-funding websites (Kickstart, Indigogo, etc.) to get a block of money in order to move forward. So now you have the cash, however, you also have to handle distribution.

With Bundle Rabbit, everything is handled via direct royalty share, as I mentioned above. That means I'm not responsible for paying my authors. (In fact, I don't ever handle money, except when I get paid my share from Bundle Rabbit at the same time everyone else does.) I do have to buy the art (and we use places like www.dreamstime.com to get quality art at a really good price). I have to spend the sweat equity to herd all my goldfish/writers, read all the stories, and assemble each issue, but only at the level of the Table of Contents. After that, it goes up and gets published. Money drips slowly in and I'm already on to the next issue.

As I was driving down to Oregon to see the eclipse in 2017, I got to talking with Fabulous Publisher Babe™ about a similar project she has been involved with for many years, The Uncollected Anthology (https://www.uncollectedanthology.com/). For them, it was originally just a collective marketing project, but more recently they have transitioned over to doing the Collaborative thing to make it easier.

But I have watched some of their issues and the growing pains they had and tried to figure out a better way. As an anarcho-communist syndicate, nobody was really in charge, and each of them took turns keeping the websites up to date, and handling various tasks. Lot of work, especially as authors have had to drop out for a time due to life and health issues. And nobody was really getting "paid" for the extra work, so it frequently came in at a lower priority to covering bills.

I decided early on that, in order to make this a magazine, I would have to step up as the editor and publisher. It would be my responsibility to do all the work (not counting whatever I could sweet-talk my wonderful wife into doing). Mostly, that involved herding goldfish. Seriously. Writers are like that. Not herding cats, mind you, because cats really only move in two dimensions. Goldfish.

I was going to have to handle all the administrative tasks. And I'm okay with that, because I used to be a Technical Project Manager in software, back in the real world. I happily kill electronic trees to defeat chaos. As recompense, that meant setting things up such that the editor/publisher would get a fixed share of the money.

At present, Bundle Rabbit takes a small, fixed fee for handling the distribution tasks. (I think 10%, but don't quote me.) After that, Knotted Road Press (my wife's publishing house, where I work as Marketing Troll), will take 25% of what comes through as our editorial fee. The remaining 75% gets split according to a slightly-complicated set of rules covered in the contract (See Appendix Two for details) and goes to all the contributors.

4

THE PITCH DOCUMENT ("WHAT'S ALL THIS THEN?")

I wanted Boundary Shock to be a pure Science Fiction magazine, published quarterly and pushing the envelope on weird. It also has to be entertaining. One of the things that got me to writing the SF that I do was that too many authors approached any given theme with an axe to grind, be it SJW, MRA, or S/RP.

I once spent three hours in the Powell's Books in Beaverton, Oregon, (not the largest one downtown, but still huge) with money in hand. I trolled up and down those massive shelves that seem to go on forever, and I could not find anything that appealed to me. Mind you, money in hand, and hours to kill. (In fact, that was the exact moment I decided I had to write the stuff I wanted to read, which turned into the novel *Auberon*. YMMV)

Nobody seemed to be writing pure, adventurous SF these days. And I'm sure part of that is that I was raised on Doc Smith, Isaac Asimov, Robert E. Howard (et al) and David Drake. Their mores and culture was alien and frequently wrong, as we judge those things today, but they all tell cracking good stories that take you on mad adventures. And they also tend to have a good moral of some sort, some lesson to be learned, but not at the expense of the storytelling.

At the same time, I have seen some anthology projects where an editor gets too detailed about their wish list, and you end up with every story being exactly alike. Maybe they left zero room for writers to play. Maybe they only like one kind of story, so that was all they would take. And maybe they demanded something so convoluted that the only way to do it was to go after the low handing fruit.

I wanted something bigger. And Weirder. We're doing SF, but I left all of the themes very broad. Here's the entire theme for Issue #3, *Grand Theft Starship*, as I sent it to the authors:

The future is not always a bright and shining beacon on a hill somewhere. Crime will follow us into space and the galaxy. What will you steal, with the whole galaxy to pick from?

That's it. Go.

The whole Release Pitch as I sent it off to folks is contained in Appendix One below, typos and everything.

On theme. With weird.

That's the challenge to the writers I wanted to recruit. Maybe they'll write horror. Maybe crime capers. Romance? Time travel? Aliens? How weird can you get, and still tell an entertaining story, with science fiction as your starting point?

So now I had an idea. My master document started out as the Release Pitch, and then I added all sorts of notes that I haven't shared with everyone, mostly because I think on paper and every odd idea gets saved there until I have a chance to think about it and decide to keep it, or toss it out.

I was going to do a quarterly Science Fiction magazine on Bundle Rabbit's Collaboration feature.

Now I needed people.

5

THE SYNDICATE

Let's face it, most modern SF (Winter 2018) is written by middle-class (frequently middle-aged) white guys. I'm no exception. There are people who aren't white guys who are writing amazingly good stuff, but they don't get enough visibility.

And that's a stupid thing.

I set out to build a group of folks by providing a platform for people who were pros, or aspired to it. I know a lot of white guys. And there are a number of them in the first Syndicate, but that's because I needed the project to turn into a thing. Once we have several issues out, I can point to it when I try to recruit more people.

When I set out, I reached out to a number of professional writers I know who have a name in science fiction. Several of them make a living at it. That was my first cut-off point, by the way. Pros known for SF.

I remember a dinner at Orycon in Nov 2017. My wife was on a panel, and was running late, so I got to entertain four of her female friends at the table until she arrived. (Fantastic ladies. Professional writers with way more experience than me.) They had heard bits of what I was up to (I was actively recruiting at that point, but quietly), and wanted all the details.

I would have loved to recruit any or all of them. All are amazing writers. However, they generally write fantasy and urban fantasy. They are all good enough that they could give me really interesting science fiction stories, on theme, with weird. But how many of their fans will cross over to read science fiction. More importantly, how much money can I get out of those fans?

I did retain all of their contact information, so that I can go back later and invite them to appear as special guest authors. I'm crazy, not stupid.

So I ended up recruiting widely, but mainly folks either who I already knew, or who had the respect of someone I trusted. And yes, I did take a few gambles in the first batch of folks, but those were calculated to bring the weird in spades. (Author's note: Holy shit did they!)

As you can see from the Release Pitch document (go read it, I'll wait…), I wanted enough material to fill a goodly sized magazine on a quarterly basis. In my mind, that was 50,000 words, give or take. Because I'm not paying by the word, I'm not really limited to only taking short work, but I didn't want novellas, so I "capped" length around 9,000 words. Most magazines want around 4-5,000, for comparison. (More Author's notes: silly me, sometimes stories have come in at 15,000+, mainly because the authors checked ahead of time and I don't care. Don't tell then that, though.)

I also wrote rules for flash, because one of the weirdoes I reached out to does flash almost exclusively. And weird flash, the best kind.

Everyone who gave me a full-length story would get a share. Flash (under 2,000 words) would get a half share, and he was good with that.

Going wider, I also put language into the contract where I could bring in visual artists. Five black-and-white sketches on theme would be a half share. Ten would be a full share, with bonus points awarded for full-color work, or putting in art we could use for a cover.

And I want poets. Gimme a five poem arc and you're a half-share. Ten-poem arc (or a lot of words, if you're Homer reincarnated) for a full share.

I have even approached some of my musician friends for sheet music, because (OMG) could you imagine a Science Fiction Rock Opera contained in some future issue?

Go weird, or go home.

Finally, I wanted to expand my horizons beyond middle-class, middle-aged white guys.

Problem: those are most of the SF writers I know.

Solution: start reaching out.

I was able to recruit four SF writers of the female persuasion (they present as female, which is good enough for me) in my initial sundicate of fourteen. Two more slots are reserved for big-name, female sf writers to join at a future point, once their current insanity abates a little bit.

This is where I hit my first recruiting problem. I was asking for semi-pro and pro writers to take on a new magazine with no track record, on a royalty-share. It's a risk. I knew that.

Several people turned me down for very legitimate reasons. I honor that. It does inspire me to make this work to the scale that they become very interested in talking to me about a slot in the syndicate at a future date, but I have a small soul.

Long term, I have contacts in places like Uganda and Nigeria who write SF in English. I want to see about getting engaged with them, possibly by sponsoring a writing prize and publishing a short list of a dozen authors under the Boundary Shock imprint. I have been talking to folks about finding Latin American authors writing SF in English. (Way too many Anglos only know Latin American literature from big, dysfunctional, family epics, or Magic Realism versions of the same.)

I'll find them, eventually, but I gotta get this thing off the ground first. So I take what I can get and recruit the folks willing to take a chance on me, my vision, and them not having to do that much work. We all understand getting access to other people's fans. That's why they submit stories to the big magazines and anthologies. Free advertising, for which they also get paid.

Getting back to length, I wanted 50,000+ words in every issue, in order to justify a pretty good price point.

To make Boundary Shock stand out a little, I also plan to have an essay in every issue on the topic at hand. I don't want a run-down of what everyone else wrote, and how it goes together. I wanted someone to tell me (and you) what the theme meant to them. Why did they write this particular story?

Each essay author will also get a full share. That means I'll get a big chunk of issue #1, however, it also gives other writers a chance to earn two shares for themselves later on. And it lets me set the stage for inviting outside folks to write non-fiction on a topic. (I plan to blackmail a lawyer friend of mine, who was there at the inception, to carry through with his threat of "How I would have done it…" one of these days.)

Long term, I want to find an academic sort of person to perhaps write me a quarterly column on "Science Fiction you should know." And I don't mean the latest flavor of the season who just got a seven figure advance for their first novel. My wife will occasionally mention some seminal book she grew up with, and how much of an impact it had on her life and her writing. And more times than not I'll look at her and go "Who?" because I came out of an entirely different place. (If you know a good historian of Science Fiction, please send them my way.)

So, I need 50,000 words, four times a year. And short fiction and essays will run around 5,000 as a nice, round number. That means I need ten stories and essays, give or take. A couple of the early members of the Syndicate immediately asked if they could write into every issue. Yes. I was already planning on doing that myself. Please join me.

So I figured that gave me 5-6 stories out of the box. I've asked everyone to write me two per year, so I need four more stories per issue, or eight people contributing. That's how I ended up at the magic number of fourteen total.

And then one of the people said "I know someone you would kill this sort of thing, and she has a huge fanbase and mailing list. Should I approach her?"

Oh Dear God, YES.

More money. More fans.

Dirty little secret for young writers just committing to try to make a living as a writer? You have a choice to make. You can be rich, or you can be famous.

Or. Not both.

Many writers want the accolades of being a famous writer, of seeing their book in the bookstore, of being invited to book signings and conventions as a guest of honor. You can make that happen. Very few of the people starting down that track today will ever make a full living at it, especially as TradPub is hemorrhaging authors and jobs these days. Fifty years ago, it was possible. Not easy, but doable. Today, not so much.

The other choice you can make is to do this for the money. I want to be Bernie Taupin. (Go read his Wikipedia entry. I'll wait…)

Everything I'm doing for Boundary Shock is geared towards expanding our fan base as wide as possible, but for greedy reasons. If your fans buy this for your new story (and I won't ever take reprints), I want them to read everyone in the issue. I can compete with anybody for story craft. You might not like my style, and that's okay. Some of your fans will find new writers they like (the reason we do this) and go buy their books as well. I want all your fans. I'm willing to share all my fans with you, and (as of this moment) I have just retired from my day job as a highly-paid database architect and business intelligence systems expert, and I'm able to live on just the money I make from my books. Note: there are no national bookstore chains I am aware of where you will find my books on the shelf. And I'm okay with that, as long as I can make money. (Hence the choice: rich or famous.)

So I recruited. There are a few names I would have liked to reach out to, and did, but they didn't know who I was (fame over money, and I was making more money than them, but didn't say that), so they didn't take the risk.

I ended the first crew with four female writers out of fifteen. And one writer of color. My long-term goal is that this represents the high-water marks for white men in Boundary Shock. I'll recruit female SF writers by preference, and POC, once I get off the ground. Because of the spectacular and well-deserved success of the Black Panther movie, there will be a number of writers of color suddenly *discovered* soon. They've always been there, kicking butt, but never got noticed. I'm hoping that I will be an outlet they will choose to work with.

All of the above is to let you know that when you go out to recruit your own syndicate, to do this on your terms, you need to identify the kind of group you want. The voices you want to see in print.

I started with professionals. That means more than just quality storytelling craft. There are a lot of writers out there who can turn a good phrase. For me, being a professional means hitting deadlines without a problem. I wanted to drop issues 1-3 over a four week stretch (Author's note: Did.), so the deadlines to get the stories to me were March 1, April 1, May 1, and June 1. Period. After that, the deadlines would go to quarterly, but I used this as a test to see who could hit that pattern, especially among the folks planning to go all in.

Then I went for different voices. Horror writers. Space Opera. Romance. Alien. *Planet Bob*. Ethical Technologist. Etc.

On theme, with weird.

So I have a Syndicate. And about an hour ago as I write this, the first deadline (issue #1) passed, and I'm looking at twelve stories.

Now, I have a month to get this issue put together and ready to go on Bundle Rabbit, before Issue #2 hits. Etc.

My next secret? I'm not reading slush piles. Open magazine or anthology calls get hundreds of stories to reject, with a few keepers. I have pros. I'll do a read-through on their doc, and perhaps format it a little for consistency, but it's going up the way they wrote it.

Being a pro means writing like one: syntax, grammar, vocabulary. These people better be pros, with the reputations they have. Or they'll destroy that reputation with crappy stories and I'll invite them to depart the Syndicate and take a Remedial English class at the local community college.

I don't exercise control over the content in the way most magazines do. Don't want it. I have my own writing career to maintain outside of this. That's the trade I'm making for speed. I have to rely on my contributors. They have to trust me to let them tell the story the way they want it done, not after I've gone and *fixed* it.

6

THE SCHEDULE (OR, INVASION OF THE MARKETING TROLL)

So at this point, I have my Syndicate in place. I've picked out the first twelve themes, which gets us through three years of releases. Now, we have to talk about the schedule. More specifically, the launch schedule and how to use it as a weapon.

Had lunch today with an old pro from the TradPub days. He wanted to pick my brain about this very project, since he had heard that I was doing something completely new and he works these days for a medium-sized game and tie-in publisher. But he's still wrapping his head around the Indie Revolution (Phase 7 began in early 2018, by the way). Still trying to figure out what it entails. He wanted to nail down some of his thoughts, against my experiences, to see if they still held. And it has lessons for you, planning to do your own collaborative magazine.

First: readers like series. Long series. Same characters over time. Comfort food, if you will. Writers who have seen sustained success these days frequently write into series, to keep their fans. Partly, this comes from the growth of episodic story-telling television as a more sophisticated medium.

Plus, readers don't want to become emotionally involved with something if it's just a one-time thing. Which leads us to the second points.

Second: reliability and predictability. In the old days, your favorite author's new novel came out in the same month, every year.

Always. TradPub did that on purpose so that readers got conditioned to expect the new hit. We're going predictable with Boundary Shock on our publishing schedule, with drops in each of January, April, July, and October. And we're going to have the same syndicate, the same cast of writers. Sure, it will evolve slowly over time, but I still expect to have roughly ten of the founders with me in five years, if all goes well and we're all making money here. Your fans will be able to pick up the next issue and expect to see many of the same faces, frequently writing into the same series or universes. Predictability.

And reliability, because we're going to do four a year for as long as I can make it work. Any special editions, year-end collections, or guest shots will be on top of that, and be driven by my success in making cash.

So how do we launch this beast?

This is where we put aside our writer hat and put on the Marketing Troll hat. Totally different way of thinking about things. Writer wants to create something new and beautiful and such. Marketing staff picks it up and says, "What the hell am I supposed to do with this?"

We want a lot of people to pick up the issues and get emotionally invested. We can do that by making sure they know from the outset that it is a series. The cover has the title and a number right there at the top. And we want to make sure they know what the Syndicate was, and how that will seed future stories.

So how do we launch this beast?

What I told the Syndicate members (Appendix One), going in, was that we would drop the first three issues back-to-back, rather than on the quarterly schedule. Early June – Late June – Early July. And not do any significant advertising push until we had issue number three out.

Then we push. Hard. "Hey, Issue Three is out. What do you mean you missed the first two? Here are links!" push. Drive home to the readers that this is the third of what is going to be a major, ongoing project. A series. Get them hooked and run with it. Tell them that issue four is coming by doing a cover reveal, because I'll already have my list of authors in hand at that point. Follow that up with a Table of Contents reveal.

And all of the authors involved in those first three issues will need to push hard on their mailing lists. (Remember, as I type this, I'm just receiving the stories for issue one, and all that I'm describing is several months out from this actually happening, so I don't know how it will turn out. That's a later chapter.) Get the word out. Drive us up the rankings on the various big players, and see how big we can make the initial splash. Make us a lot of money.

But there's a big caveat to all of that. *Big Launch Days* are a TradPub thing. They've become accustomed (perhaps addicted is a better term) to that first big week of sales, and measure the success of any author purely on the sales they can record in the first seven days. Careers have bene ended for not hitting those numbers on the first novel in the first week.

For you, the Indie Author, you aren't forced to submit to that model. The first, big, week is nice, but you don't have to follow the artificial scarcity model. I'm putting these things up for as long as possible (read: forever). They can earn us money forever, as well.

The reason we will put three up in short order is to hook the readers on having a series from the get-go. And because we're going for a long run, we can keep recruiting fans, who will go back to the beginning, even years later. This is the long-tail of publishing.

This is your job. If you want to make it a career, you need to get used to things on long intervals. I regularly see sudden spikes in my old series, because some robot somewhere tossed book one into some advertising loop, and suddenly lots of people see it. The same will happen with this, doubly so since we'll regularly feed the beast.

7

THE NEXT STEPS

So, as I'm writing this (early March 2018), I have received all the stories for issue one. And now I'm starting to remind folks about issue two deadlines in four weeks. And issue three right behind that. And issue four right behind that.

The work never stops, but it will get crazy for the next five or six months, until we're over the first hump and I can shift people onto the quarterly schedule.

Now, I'm into the production process of issue one. If you have never built an anthology, there are some things you need to think about. I'm not giving you the Gospel, but here is how I go about doing this, based on having done several in the past. So I'll dedicate the next few chapters to fleshing these steps out. If you have done this, you might shake your head at my approach, and you might learn some things, but you will need to find your own way to do these things.

First and perhaps foremost is to figure out how to organize yourself. I use excel spreadsheets to track each issue, so I know what authors are planning to write in. I also can track which stories I have received. And one I do my reading, I can assign a genre, a theme, and a color to every story. We'll cover that more in the next chapter.

Not everyone does it this way, and you don't have to, but YOU MUST BE ORGANIZED. I have worked with an editor that honestly thought he could keep the entire anthology in his head. I won't work with that editor again. Ever. (And neither will anyone else, as he's burned a number of publishers and they talk over beer.)

Another thing you have to do now is to read the stories. As the publisher, I have to build the anthology emotionally, so I need to know what each story is and where it should go, relative to the others.

Covers and branding is also an important consideration, because I want my readers to immediately recognize the brand, especially if they missed an issue and need to catch up.

What else? Lots, but we'll cover that in later chapters.

So, with that in mind, let's move on to the editorial and publishing process.

8

ORGANIZING YOURSELF

You'll note that I don't call this Organizing Your Magazine/Anthology. We're not there yet. First, you have to organize yourself. I'll use myself as an example, and then ask my wife to use herself as a counter-example. You need to know that there lots of different ways to do this. Find the one that works for you.

To start, I created a folder on my computer and backups, so everything went into its place. Boundary Shock folder. Most docs and spreadsheets inside that at the top level. Sub-folders for each issue, as I needed them tracked. Other sub-folders for things like copies of contracts I mined, and signed final contracts I got from my Syndicate. Good to go.

I started this project by building up a long and messy word document with bulleted lists of things, mostly just whiteboarding on paper. Any thought that might be appropriate, useful, or needed further investigation went in. Only later did I start putting them into some grouped lists, so I could start identifying gaps, as well as strengths.

How did I want to do this? What themes should we explore? How about annuals and special issues? Did we want to do a collective, or an editor/publisher model? Etc.

Once I had a few pages of notes, I started a second document that would become the Release Pitch. Get the details down, and write them well enough that a complete stranger could look at them, understand, and make an informed decision as to whether or not they wanted to join. Remember, about half the people I tried to recruit turned me down, frequently flat, because it didn't fit into their current career path. That's okay.

You are responsible for your own career. Let me repeat that.

You are responsible for your own career.

If this doesn't sound like a good fit for where you want to be in a year, don't do it. Perhaps reserve the right to circle back later, but we all have our plans and I was asking people to change them on a semi-risky proposition.

Once I had the Release Pitch done (and that took several tries, as I thought of new things, bounced ideas off some trusted folks, and got their feedback), then I started to reach out to science fiction writers I didn't know as well, but who I considered to be professionals. No slush. No amateurs. No dilettantes. I'm lucky to be part of the Oregon Writers Network (OWN), so I know pros, and more importantly, they know me. We could talk. They could trust that I knew which end of the pencil worked. (Usually.)

As I started reaching out to these writers, I started a list. My list was bulleted, and showed their name, in the order I had reached out, and their current status: want to contact, sent Pitch, accepted/rejected. I had a long list of names to contact, and in my head I had their characteristics and fan base, so I didn't need that on paper, but I was only aiming for 10-14 people, so I could do that mentally at that level. Horror writer. Romance writer. Hard SF. Space Fantasy.

Organization. You must have it written down, or you will forget it. I promise.

Then, as they accepted, I moved them into a spreadsheet and asked them which of the first twelve issues (3 years) they thought sounded like fun, assuming two stories per year. Now I have a pulse for which issues are likely to be heavy, and which light. If I have ten stories, I'm happy. If I have an issue with only six planned, I either need to invite in a special guest, or, more likely, write a second story myself or ask one of these pros for a favor and an extra share.

Finally, as those first stories came in, I had my Issue One list: who was planning to send me a story; has the story come in; what theme and sub-genre is it? Because it is a spreadsheet, that's a column, so I can track these things over time. (I'm like that. YMMV)

These are my examples of how I do things. Find the one that works for you, but it must be organized. You have to be able to lay hands on any piece of information immediately, not after pawing through the piles on your desk, and eventually finding it taped to the cat. I expect my writers to act like professionals, organized and on-time. They expect me to reciprocate.

I expect you to, as well.

Fabulous Publisher Babe

Honestly, most everything that Blaze has said works for me. You must be organized with this sort of project, from the very start.

And that means keeping your materials together and sorted on your computer, as well as developing spreadsheets for production.

Because I run Knotted Road Press, and I do most of the production work, I've developed systems for naming things. As Blaze said, YMMV. But I would strongly consider the following:

Come up with a naming scheme for all of your blurbs. For example, ALL of my blurbs are contained in files that start with the word INFO. That way, when I look in the folder for a particular project, I can tell at a glance if I've created that file or not.

Use separate file folders for everything, then name them consistently as well. For example, I put all the cover files in a folder called title_Cover (with title being the title of the book). Similarly, I have folders always named title_Edits, title_Audio, and so on. You get the picture.

One of the things Blaze hasn't mentioned is keeping track of your metadata, such as the keywords you use for a title. I use a separate spreadsheet for that. The reason? Some distributors, namely Amazon, regularly change their categories and keywords. Categories that used to be there no longer are. Having a single place where you can check and see what keywords you used for a title will really help if you have to change it all.

Create a production spreadsheet/checklist. I have many steps that I need to finish before I publish something, such as create the ebook cover, create the print cover, write the blurb, create the Facebook header, and so on. Keep yourself organized not just in the pre-production phase but the actual production phase as well.

Spreadsheet of links. I have a single spreadsheet where I keep all the links to all the books I've ever published. It makes it much, much easier to do something with a book if you have all that information already gathered and at hand.

9

BUILDING YOUR ANTHOLOGY

Now, the hard part. And the fun part. And the crazy part.

You'll have perhaps a dozen stories by different people, writing in different sub-genre, with radically different interpretations of your theme. My themes are intended to be loose enough to get all manner of stories. I already know it's going to get weird. And I'm not looking to tell the same story from seven different angles. Yuck.

Now you have to read the stories. Curating an anthology is where the magic happens. Figure out what each story is about. How is it going to impact the reader emotionally?

In an anthology, I usually identify five "slots" into which stories should be put. Note: twelve stories, five slots. This is not a 1:1 thing.

I want you to think of making a mixtape for someone you have a crush on. This makes more sense that way, 'cause we've all done something that silly at some point. (Yes, you.)

First, and most important, is the Opening Story (or Song). This is the one that your reader will find when they crack the spine. In an online preview, this is the ten percent that they read to decide if they want to buy. Your crush puts the tape in and starts listening. Make sure you got them hooked, right out of the gate.

Returning to stories for now, this needs to be your strongest candidate. Not necessarily the best, but absolutely the one that establishes the tone for the anthology. If you have nine stories that are dark, heavy, and emotional, you do not want to lead with the only cute, bubbly, kitten story you have, because the reader will be expecting cute and bubbly, and you will piss them off. Forever. I don't care if it is the greatest kitten story ever written. You're selling them a pig in a poke.

So find that story that is the emotional heart of your anthology. The one that sets the mood you want. Lead with it, because you need to get your reader into the collection at this point. The entire book will be an emotional rollercoaster if you've done your job, so tell them what kind of ride it is going to be with your first story.

For me, the second most important thing is to identify the story I want to end on. The last one. How do you want them to come out the back? In one anthology I did, I had only one dark, heavy, angry story, but one that was amazingly well-told. It was going to piss off a lot of people, and I knew that. It went last, because I was certain that many people would never even make it through that subject matter, and I wanted everyone else to be seen. And if you did make it, you had an emotional punch to the stomach, the sort that stayed with you for a long time.

So, now you have both ends of the anthology. The story that will lead people in, and then send them on their way, happy and snug.

At the center of the anthology, you need to look at putting your third best story. Right at the hump. I'll come back later with more details as to the why. First, I want to talk about the other two spots of our original five.

After your lead story, and perhaps a couple more of the good ones, you have the first place where you can bury things. Stories that were okay, but not fantastic. Adequate. Good enough to be included, but not the best stories you got. This is where you separate the amazing from the good. Because they had to be good to be included here, right?

Perhaps you have a good story with a completely different theme or emotional resonance from the rest. Going back to the original example, nine dark stories and our kittens. The kitten story stands out from the rest. If it is a great story, you could put it into this first spot, as a bit of relief from the dark stuff.

The other spot you might put stories that stick out from the rest are after the middle story. Buried in a back corner, as it were, but not at the very back, because the last story is the one you want the reader to remember. If it is a bad one, they'll remember the whole anthology as a bad effort and not recommend it.

So in spots two and four (of five) are where we put the ones that are less amazing or less of an overall fit. In between them, right at the middle, we need to insert our third best story.

So far, they have gotten on the rollercoaster, and taken off. You've pulled them in with the lead, and held them with the second (and maybe third), and then given them a couple that maybe weren't quite as good. At the middle slot, you remind them that this is a good anthology. Hit them with another story that pushes them emotionally back into the place where you led off.

Remember: rollercoaster. Emotional highs and lows.

You want the reader thrilled and scared. Panicked and going "awwwwwww." Then you bring them back to center for a story, before taking them into the fourth slot, which is where the really weird, "what the hell do I do with this story?" stories go. Kittens in an anthology about plague and apocalyptic riders. But an amazing story about kittens. Run with it. Smack the reader upside the head with a four-days-rotting sand shark, just because you can.

Last and not least, send them on their way with that second-best story we talked about before. Contrasted with the kittens, you'll have readers tell other people "Oh. My. God. You have to read this thing!!!"

So there you have it. Five slots into which I categorize work when I'm building an anthology. Other editors have their own ways to do it. Find your own way, but understand that you are building your own personal mixtape, with the dozen stories you have in hand. Ups and downs. Loves and hates. OMG, I can't breathe.

Whatever works for you to convey the secret sauce.

10

TECHNICAL MATTER

Because we want you to look like a professional, there are always certain pages and sections you must include in your magazine. Perhaps the most important of these is the cover, which we will go through in the chapter after this. Now, I want to talk about the interior, technical matter.

Personally, I think it would be most helpful if you went and bought a copy of Boundary Shock Quarterly so you had a workbook to open and follow along at home. I'll wait…

Good? Okay.

At the beginning of the print edition, you want the copyright page. Note, I said print edition. For the eBook, you want it dead last. They go different places in the two versions of consumption. Traditionally, everyone expects them at the front of a paper book. But in an eBook, the savvy reader is going to open for the ten percent (or whatever) free material. You want story in front of them, not copyright.

So, on that page, include your copyright information, publisher with website, ISBN number if you have one, artwork copyright (because it will be different and should be under a license of some sort), and all your legal boilerplate. Go look at something put out by a Major or Traditional publisher for an idea of what you need.

On that same page, include the title, © 2018 (or appropriate year) and the author's name for each story. I am not claiming any ownership of these stories. I am merely licensing them with an exclusive for several months, followed by an on-going, non-exclusive license. All authors retain full rights to their material, unlike many TradPub deals.. (See the contact in Appendix Two, specifically the *AGREEMENT* Section 1-12 for a pretty good idea. I am not a lawyer, and this is not legal advice. Consult a legal expert if you have questions. Got it?)

After that, the Table of Contents. Show them who's involved, and wow them with the list of "Oh, wow. She's in here, too?" They won't be able to consume them until they buy it, so you can tease them with what they haven't seen. Remember, your second best story should be last, so they can see who it will be, but money must change hands to get it.

Then all your stories go in.

For me, at the end of each author's story, I'm including a line like this: *For more information, visit Blaze Ward's Author page on www.boundaryshockquarterly.com.* And the whole thing is a hyperlink back to that author's personal page on the Boundary Shock Quarterly website.

I'm using a tool called Mooberry Book Manager (MBM), with the add-on module MBM Multi-Author. Each issue gets a page, showing all the authors in it. Each author gets a page showing all the issues that they are in. If you are gonna do this sort of thing, I'm not the only person who will tell you these products are worth the investment.

By sending the reader to the Author's page, it also lets the author keep their details up to date in one place, which is good. Remember reading something ten years old and laughing at how dated things are. Here, I just bring them in, and then from the author's page they can be bounced out to whatever place the author desires.

What I have told my authors is to include a brief bio, possibly a picture (or representative pictogragh), and then links to their webpage and any and all social media locations where they can be followed easily. (And Patreon or other crowd-funding links.) Remember, this is all about the collaborative marketing effect.

Now, we get to the weird parts.

At the back of the book, I have the following pages added as something of a template.

First is the Boundary Shock logo page. Our logo, our website, and our mission statement: "The Science Fiction you want to read." Nothing else, just a reminder of what this is, who we are, and what it is all about.

After that, next issue's Cover Reveal. I already know what the next issue will be, and I'll have the art done as a good mockup, because I'm working at least a year out for the art. I won't know who the authors are in that issue, so that area will be listed as TBA. If I do know who I have invited to write the essay, I will include that.

After that, because I can: For each issue of Boundary Shock I have a back page ad on the print edition. (It will go inside, towards the rear of the eBook, for obvious reasons.) For the first several issues, I do not plan to charge people, and have invited organizations I like to put in a full page advertisement for free. Obviously, there's technically no back page on an eBook, so we place that same ad after the cover reveal page of the eBook. I like these people, and want them to succeed, so free space.

Later, I'll target organizations with a marketing budget and charge them for space. Not sure how much, right now. Too much depends on the heft of the magazine (both physical and mind-share) when we get there. However, my plan, when I do start charging people for space, is to reduce the share that the editor takes of the overall royalty-share money, since I will have recouped some of my expenses before the issue ever goes live. My authors can then get more of the sales dollars in their own pockets.

Our Friends is a section at the very back, after the ad, where I list people I like, doing things I approve of. In the eBook, this includes links so you can find them. In print, the name will have to do, but I'll also have a similar page on the website.

After that, Last-But-Not-Least, for the eBook edition only, do we include the copyright page. At the end, out of the way of the 10% preview feature.

11

BRANDING AND COVERS

So we've got the interior built. Time to talk Branding and Covers.

In Boundary Shock, I could cheat on this topic, because I had a theme for every issue. If you do the same, then you need to find a cover that conveys accurately to the prospective reader what we're all about.

Issue #1: Captain's Log. I chose that deliberately, because so many of us know those words, and they take us to a place immediately. So let's talk about the cover and how it builds the brand.

Across the top the words Boundary Shock, with the logo and the issue number. So this is a thing, and it is part of a sequence. Some future reader will accidentally wander into the room with Issue #7. They'll know that it is a 7.

The Modern Speculative Fiction Magazine

We're trying to convey seriousness here, and let you know that this is all about a more literary version of old-fashioned science fiction. You're going to get professional stories (I hope).

Everything else was on black, so now white background with black letters draw the eye to what this issue contains. "Captain's Log." Boom. We're going space exploration, on a big ship, against a weird and possibly hostile galaxy.

And in case you missed it, the picture is a woman wearing a spacesuit, staring back at you. Hopefully, none of you are confused and expecting splatter horror at this point.

Stories By: Hey, look! There's a story by my all-time favoritest writer in here. And that other lady! And him!

Comfort food, for fans looking forward to their next hit from their favorite weirdo.

Finally, the essay. I have chosen to include an essay on the topic by someone, every issue. And not (usually) a recap of the issue. What I have challenged people to write is "Why I wrote this story." Or "What this topic means to me." It is not necessary, for your average anthology, but I want people to think of this as a literary SF magazine. I mentioned the plans for columns earlier, as well as going beyond the mere written word. I wanna go big, and weird, and impressive.

We could go on forever about covers and branding, but this is not the space. Take some classes and learn how to do it. But understand that this is now a series. You need a cover that conveys brand, and a brand that communicates genre and intent. It's more than just slapping a picture and some words up. It is all about the font and the placement of the letters, even the kerning. The flow of the entire thing from top to bottom and left to right.

Subtle cues that will make someone stop on the website when they see the postage-stamp-sized thumbnail and go "Hey, what's that?" Or, better, "When did I miss issue #7????"

Hope that helps. I have to stop writing now and put this book away. For you reading at home, it's March and I have all of Issue #1's stories in hand. I'm starting out on the reading, building, and covers.

12

WEBSITE AND SOCIAL MEDIA

Small time gap from the last chapter. My apologies if this feels a little rough, but I'm writing as I go, rather than trying to go back and remember everything after the fact. That's a good way to forget things.

On the drive to the eclipse, the first thing we did as we started bouncing names off the wall was to find something that conveyed Big Space Stories and was free as a domain name. I have no idea why an architecture firm has the short domain, but they do as I write this, and it is a parked domain that points on to their completely-unrelated main page.

But we were able to locate www.boundaryshockquarterly.com and buy it immediately. I cannot emphasize this enough Once you have a short list of working names, go make sure that nobody else isn't already using one. Do a search in the internet and see what hits you get.

Nobody was using Boundary Shock in anything remotely related to Science Fiction. Several of the other ideas we had were close enough to other people for confusion and possible lawsuits. Screw that.

So I have the domain. I used Blue Host to park my domains, with privacy turned on. (When someone does a "whois" search, they won't get all my personal information. If you are a woman and own a domain, turn that shit on immediately. Guys, give it good consideration and have a reason not to. Too many stalker, trolls, and shit-heads out there to waiting for a chance to dox you.)

Dropped a WordPress site in place. My wife, the Fabulous Publisher Babe™ is an expert on WordPress, and I've gotten pretty good at keeping it up to date.

The list of plugins that we use on BoundaryShockQuarterly.com currently are:

Jetpack: a collection of tools that are used by every WordPress site.

Wordfence Security: protects your site from being low-level hacked. The free version is adequate protection for your site to start with. As you become more well known you may need to upgrade.

Updraft Plus: a free backup program. Backup your websites. There is no excuse not to.

MailerLite Forms: we use MailerLite for our newsletter at this time, so we use their forms for newsletter signups.

WPForms Lite: used to create the form on our privacy policy.

Mooberry Book Manager and **MBM Multi-Author**: used to create the book catalog as well as the author pagers.

Finally, Mooberry Dreams has two tools: Mooberry Book Manager and the add-on module MBM Multi-Author. Book Manager lets me easily set up a bunch of different books and track them easily. MBM is designed to make it easy for one book to have more than one author. So, anthology/magazine, and I can link each author page to all the different issues that they appear in. And, conversely, each issue can be linked to all the authors who appear inside.

Trust me, I can hand-code html, and do every once in a while, when necessary. Mooberry Dreams makes my life so much easier. If you only ever plan to write one or two books, don't bother. If you plan to make writing a job and a career, talk to Christie. She will save you a lot of headache. And do it now, rather than having to go back and fix everything later.

The following is the general layout of the website:

Main Page/Welcome

Who are we?

What are we up to?

No, we don't take submissions

Publishing Schedule with dates (including fake backwards dates you are lying about)

Letters to the editor

Author Pages

Each author has a page. In each issue, I have a hyperlink to that page, so they can control the message easily and refresh it as appropriate. As the publisher, I think you'll be well-served to do something similar.

For each page, quick bio. Two hundred words max. DO NOT LET THEM TALK ABOUT THEIR CATS, unless they write kitty mystery cozies. I'm publishing a speculative fiction magazine, so I want your professional credentials (because you are all professionals here). Awards you have won. Series you have written. Other places the reader can find you books. Sound like a pro.

Second, I wanted a picture. Or close-enough pictographic representation. Not all of my current crop of writers are identifiable from their picture. That's okay. It still make you appear both more professional and more personal.

IMPORTANT PART HERE: include all the links out they want. Their website. Their various social media links. Their Patreon/micro-funding sites. The works. As publisher, you want to drive readers from the magazine to exactly this page, so make it sticky. Mooberry lets the reader then ask the magical question: "What other issues of Boundary Shock is this person in? I need to buy them."

Do not make it hard for the reader to give you more money, you fool!

Keep the author pages up to date. Poke your lazy goldfish writers to review and send you updates at least annually. We want things to look professional. That is your job, and part of the reason you get an editor's share of the money.

Newsletter signups and the blog

Give your readers an easy way to sign up for the newsletter. You want them engaged.

I shouldn't have to say this to professionals, but make it clear that you will not sell their personal information on to third party vendors, and that you won't spam them.

And don't. (GDPR came into play between then and now, and things can get nasty now, too.)

Publish your expected schedule on the page and try to hold to it. If that's weekly, they'll know what they are getting into. I try to do a personal newsletter on a quarterly schedule, because I aim to blog three weeks in four about less important tasks.

For Boundary Shock, I plan to send the newsletter monthly. Pub dates are targeted on the tenths of months (never a set holiday, as near as I can tell), so I would send out the "did you see/buy?" reminder at the beginning of the next month. After that, the cover reveal in an issue. Then the Table of Contents reveal.

Eyes = money.

In the shorter terms, I'll set up a blog and invite people to send me things to post. For my authors, why did they write this story? Or: what does it mean? For me, technical challenges: where am I on the next issue. What surprises are in store?

Finally, for fans, I will allow something along the lines of letters to the editor, heavily screened. This doesn't mean only the good ones, but only the polite ones. I don't mind you calling me a fool, if your syntax and grammar are up to snuff. Your complaint about some issue or story might be the impetus for other readers to go back and decide that maybe they should have bought it.

Publicity = money.

13

HOW TO COLLABORATE ON
THE BUNNY

At present (Spring 2018, and it will change), the process for doing a curated anthology/magazine on Bundle Rabbit has a number of steps you have to go through. And will have to go through every time, but it should get easier once the goldfish all have done it a few times.

Dividing Up Shares

Before you do anything, time for math. In Boundary Shock, I normally take a twenty-five percent cut for the editorial process. I have to pay artists, designers, and employees out of that, but I get my money at the same time everyone else does, and not first.

As I may have mentioned elsewhere (and I'm writing this out of order, so maybe it's in the future), I have the back cover in print and the end of the eBook, where I am offering people I like advertising space. Initially, I'm offering it for free to some orgs doing good work. Later, I plan to charge an up-front, fixed amount to put your ad in the issue. When I get money in, my plan is to reduce the percentage the editor takes, and provide a bigger pool for all the writers in that issue.

So now you have to *Math*. One Hundred Percent (100%), minus my quarter (or less, depending). Remaining pool evenly divided among all writers who put a story or essay into the issue. Half-share for flash. If someone writes a story and an essay, two shares.

Do this on a spreadsheet, because that's way easier.

I round to the quarter percent. For example, in Issue One, it worked out to 6.5% and 3.25%, respectively, and the editor actually ended up taking 25.25%. (And I didn't count my essay against total shares for this issue, because I wanted everyone else to get that extra half percent. I want happy writers.)

You'll need these numbers at your fingertips in the next section. Save yourself the headache and do it now. And make sure it adds up to one hundred percent, because you have to have an exact sum when we get there or the computer throws a fit.

Setting Things Up/Phase One

First, everyone in your syndicate needs to sign up for accounts on Bundle Rabbit. Period. Non-negotiable. If they wanna be mistaken for pros, they need to act like it. Signed up, linked to their payment account so Bundle Rabbit can send them money. The works.

Second, they have to tell you which email address they used to sign up. I have seven different email accounts (I think), so it can be messy, but the writer only uses two of them, well demarcated, so easy to track.

Third, as the editor/publisher, Knotted Road Press has its own log-in, so that money can be distributed cleanly, with shares directly to editor and shares directly to writers, and no co-mingling of funds. (An accounting no-no and nightmare waiting to be audited.)

Now the messy bits.

You, the curator of the magazine, will log into Bundle Rabbit and create a new curation project. Give it a name (Boundary Shock 001) that makes it easy to track and alphabetize.

Invite your editor in, by the exact email they used, and assign them the share you expect them to get. Hit send.

This is where them not already having created an account makes a lot of work for you. Because if that email is not in the system, you generate a "Please sign up to Bundle Rabbit so I can invite you into this bundle" email. And then wait for them to go through that process before you can proceed.

If they have set it up, they get an invitation that they can accept. (And you see them go from No to Yes.)

Once everyone has accepted (and this will take a while with the first few issues), and everything adds up to EXACTLY 100%, you can lock the participants and proceed on to Phase Two.

Phase Two

When you have **locked** participation in this issue, everyone must review the contract and accept it in order to participate in THIS ISSUE ONLY. You, the editor, will need to send everyone a reminder to log in to Bundle Rabbit, where they should see a new reminder/advisory on their dashboard to look at the collaboration contract. When you click the reminder, it will take them to the list of participants for the collaboration. On the line with their name, they have to find the buttons on the far right. The buttons are kinda confusing (we're working on that), but they will need to click the [CONTRACT] button, read it all (Yes, READ IT, always read contracts and agree with them before proceeding), and click *I accept* at the bottom of the page (assuming).

This is Bundle Rabbit's contract, not mine. My contract with the syndicate earlier was rules for play. I have no control over this language, and if someone wants to back out at this point, we have a problem, but not an insurmountable one.

If someone really decides that they can't be part of this, based on Bundle Rabbit's contract language, you will have to unlock the collaboration and remove the person who won't be playing. Then it will be necessary to recalculate and reset shares to add back up to one hundred percent, before you can relock participants and start Phase Two over.

As a side note, the first time someone does that to me without a DAMNED GOOD EXCUSE, I will be excusing them from the Syndicate. Permanently. There are a lot of other ways they could have handled things, long before this, that would have appeared more professional. Something has gone wrong in a legal sense and they hoped they would be able to fix it before things got out of hand.

So, once there are no problems and everyone accepts, you are finished with Phase Two. You will probably have to hound your goldfish repeatedly until everyone accepts, because this step blocks everything else.

Unlike Phase One, where you get an email every time someone accepts the contract, you, the editor, will need to log in regularly and check. Do so.

Phase Three

The writers are done now. They have finished all their tasks, and it's back to you, the editor.

First, you need to generate the final editions of all your documents (eBooks, print, etc.).

Then, make sure you have your blurb and meta-data written down ahead of time in a separate document, because you'll have to enter it several times, in slightly different ways each time, because each distributor has differing requirements and needs.

Now you have to log into the Rabbit and set up the sales channels individually. (I'll refer you to Chuck's book and save myself repeating him.)

Right now, you have Amazon, Kobo, iTunes, Barnes & Noble, and Createspace (print). The meta-data tends to be similar, and sometimes gets remembered, but you have to set up each issue for each channel, and the answers are different.

This will take a while. Budget a couple of hours to do this, maybe a half day. This is a task. It will require significant effort to complete.

It is now June 2018, and I've put the first three issues up for pre-order. By the third one, it was taking me about 90 minutes to complete, but I will have forgotten most of this by the time I get back to loading Issue 004, so I'll just plan on a half-day at the library doing this.

One of the weird things coming is the need to set your base price and then for all the currencies currently available. The system will offer a bunch of suggested prices in various currencies, which you will need to go through and set. They also explain some of the logic of pricing, based on cultural mores. It is a long list, and you will need to fill in all the boxes individually.

When you are done, you have one last choice to make. Publish immediately, or set it up for pre-order.

I do the pre-order thing, because I want the various issues to always drop on the tenth of the target month. Personal preference, you can do whatever you want.

However, print edition becomes available about a week after you submit, because the systems at Bundle Rabbit have to do their thing, and then the robots at Createspace (and later the new thing Amazon will replace it with, which might be called Kindleprint) take a few days.

But that's it.

14

MARKETING

It's now published (or available for pre-order). You should celebrate.

And then go claim it, if necessary for your author page (think: Amazon). This is part of the reason I also do the pre-order, so I have time to claim it and hopefully Amazon and others will send out notice emails to everyone who has signed up that I have a new title available for pre-order.

Now comes the marketing part. On your dashboard, you should be able to see the URLs to the various distributors, as they are. Please note that (as of now), each link will show an Affiliate code at the end.

As the publisher, you have the choice to send the exact link as is to all of your authors, or you can strip off Bundle Rabbit's affiliate code and insert your own instead. (If you don't know what any of this means, don't worry and just send the links as is. Some folks nerd out on this sort of thing.)

To each of your authors, you should send the complete list of links, along with reminders of when the issue is going live, so they can start putting their own marketing plans into action. This will need to go out to my social media. I'll put it into the Boundary Shock newsletter that I'm going to send a few weeks later, so the fans can jump right to it and give me money. It will go in my personal, quarterly newsletter with a "Did you miss?" tag.

Remember, the whole point of this task is money.

Boundary Shock is a collaborative marketing exercise that I hope ends up making me lots of money, but at least exposes me to lots of everyone else's fans.

So, marketing. Early in 2018. That means I should set up a Facebook group page for Boundary Shock Quarterly.

Invite your syndicate to join the group. Include that link in all your others, so on the main page of your website. And on your personal website. And your newsletters and blog posts. Ask your authors to include it in their marketing materials.

Every issue, make sure your Art Department comes up with a new Facebook header for the page, so that you can remind people that the new issue is out and looks cool.

I plan (future tense) to post on the Facebook group page regularly, and to let the various writers and fan interact. We'll want to post interviews, blogs, ideas, stories, etc. there, to drive traffic in and out.

In a similar vein, I'll be posting blogs and pictures and stuff on the Boundary Shock Quarterly website on a regular basis, and asking my folks to give me things to add. And asking them to advertise the newsletter sign-up, so we build a separate mailing list for the magazine.

What do you normally do to push a new book release? Do it here. Simple as that.

Next section starts up this summer, after I have dropped those first three issues, so I can talk about how the process worked.

See you soon.

15

AND HOW DID IT GO (SUMMER)?

I appear to have remained relatively sane, compared to where I was ten months ago, on a drive down to Oregon to watch an eclipse. Issue 001 (Captain's Log) came out about two weeks ago as I write these words. Issue 002 (Tuesday After Next) comes out Tuesday, which I picked because it is my birthday. Issue 003 is up for preorder and has been processed everywhere.

There was an issue from Createspace with the print cover for 003. Text too close to the edge of the page. Fabulous Publisher Babe™ fixed it quickly and sent Bundle Rabbit a new version, which they were able to process through.

I have my brag-shelf copies of Issue 001 in hand. 002 has been shipped. 003 is on order.

I have not yet read my stories for Issue 004, but that's because I forced the schedule when setting everything up, and built in slack for myself on the back. Plus, several of my pros reached out and asked if they could come in late, because life happened.

They are professionals. They communicated to me. I can be very flexible, because I presumed goldfish and left myself (and them) wiggle room. I'll be back to civilization from CampCon in a few days and then I can read everything.

So what did Year One look like?

Issue 001 came in at 12 stories and my essay.

Issue 002 came in at 11 stories and Joel's literary analysis of maker culture (wow, by the way).

Issue 003 (which I expected to be the heaviest of the first four for participation) came in at 7 stories and an essay, which made me nervous, right up until I counted words. Leah and ChuckA were both over 16,000 words with their stories. (I'm not paying by the word, and this is FlashFictionChuck going even weirder than normal on me. Seriously.)

All of the first three issues came in just north of 70,000 words, which it a pretty damned good bargain for $4.99 ebook. That's in the nice novel range. 004 is probably longer. (Author's Note: yup. 90,000)

Issue 004, which I have not read yet, came in at 14 stories and an essay, which means everybody but one wrote a story for **Robots, Cyborg, Androids, Oh My!**

Next comes the hard push for marketing in a few weeks, once issue 003 drops, and we can convince the average reader that we're serious business with an ongoing series of issues that can afford to get addicted to.

Just looked at Amazon and there are no reviews for Issue 001, but "Readers also bought" Issue 002, so we're off. Money will start flowing into my author's pockets in about 90-120 days, depending on Amazon and Bundle Rabbit's robots.

Of my original fourteen recruits to join, a couple of them wrote into every issue. Everybody but one contributed two stories, which was the minimum requirement for continued membership in the Syndicate.

So what's next?

I have reached out to a number of people, to line up Special Guest Appearance By… names for Year Two. I'm trying to avoid the Cis White Male as a writer demographic, unless someone awesomely amazing comes along. So far, I have talked to four people, with two firm commitments at present. All of them are female (or at least present that way).

I'm reaching out to a wider group of folks to see who I might be able to recruit to fill slots in the Syndicate as they open.

And more importantly, there is this document, which (I hope) might walk you through the process by which you could decide to create your own genre magazine. There is no secret sauce, beyond the will on your part to go beyond being a writer and decide to turn yourself into a publisher.

That is not an easy thing, and most writers never want to do it, or do it once and then discover how much hard work is involved in herding all the goldfish and making all the decisions.

If this is for you, then congratulations. And best of luck.

16

AND IN CONCLUSION...

This the trip I made in getting to the point where I could publish the first three issues of <u>Boundary Shock Quarterly</u> magazine. Issue 004 is in process as we speak, but will have long since come out by the time most of you read these words.

That's okay, I'm trying to write this in the present tense, rather than going back afterwards and trying to remember things.

As I read through the old stuff, I had to make a couple of serious revisions, because in one of them I talked about the original cover I had chosen for Issue 001, before a couple of my writers suggested something else, which turned out to be our actual, final cover.

In another area, I had done something with issue 001, and then the folks at Vellum made a change with one of their updates to the software, and broke what I had done. The original plan was to have the Table of Contents (by that name) at the front, and then include an exact copy of it at the end of the stories, so readers didn't have to flip back. The change Vellum made was to have the TOC only show stuff after it falls into the final doc, so I ended up with just the back matter listed. Took me two days to figure that one out. Kept thinking I had done something wrong.

Nope.

But I have persevered. Starting with Appendix One, right behind this, I have included the Release Pitch that I sent out to prospective writers, when I was trying to recruit folks for my Syndicate. I have included the typos and other mistakes. If you decide to copy it, please fix them, and then erase everything, because you will be doing your own thing and the only part that will probably help you is the actual format, which you could use as a template to create your own.

Why not do a monthly romance magazine? Or a Crime Quarterly? The technology is there for anyone to use and Indie writers need more avenues to successful discoverability.

Appendix Two is one you should study closer. That is the actual contract I signed with all my Syndicate players. It is an amalgam of several of the good contracts I have ever encountered, and some of the folks I talked to suggested improvements. I am not a lawyer, and this is not legal advice. What it represents is a very clear understanding between me as editor/publisher, and my writers. And I signed one myself, as well, because I might sell the whole shebang off, one of these days, and want someone else to take over the magazine portion.

It has been a fantastically fun journey for me, to create something I have always wanted to do, and hold it in my hands, with an expectation that this magazine will continue for many years, making us money and fame (in that order) and letting us all have fun.

It is hard work. But it is rewarding, if you get professionals. Remember, the Syndicate is only as good as the people you fill it with, so much of your success will rest on their shoulders, and pick accordingly.

But I wouldn't have changed much, knowing what I do today.

shade and sweet water
blaze
west of the mountains, WA

17

APPENDIX ONE: THE RELEASE PITCH

Below is the actual release pitch document I used to recruit my initial group of authors. This version dates to February 2018, which is about the time everyone was starting to deliver their stories to me.

18

BOUNDARY SHOCK QUARTERLY/
BUILDING THE SYNDICATE

"On theme. With weird."

The Pitch

I'm creating a quarterly Science Fiction magazine called *Boundary Shock*, where I will be the principle editor and publisher.

It will be published out of Bundlerabbit.com, which is run by a friend of mine and a (hopeful) member of the Syndicate. Using the 'Rabbit allows me to manage important things and then let Chuck worry about the logistics of paying people every month, which will be easy because he has already built the tools to handle it.

In addition, the collaborator function on Bundlerabbit lets me pay both authors and editors a share of overall income automatically by splitting things up ahead of time. This will be important as the back catalog grows and each issue has a different cast that has to be paid on a regular and evolving basis.

In order to make sure the magazine has legs, I want to first build up a group of creatives called ***The Syndicate***. This is more than just writers, as people could easily contribute art and poetry, as well as more-typical genre fiction and whatever else we can come up with. Membership in the Syndicate allows you to write into any issue of Boundary Shock that strikes your fancy, with an expectation that you will plan to be in at least two issues every year (life rolls notwithstanding).

Because this is done via Bundlerabbit, we are on a royalty-share model, so there is no money up front. This lets me keep my expenses down and recoup my time and effort over a longer horizon. It also lets me do this without having to do kickstarts, fund-raisers, or subscriptions, although I reserve the right to do any and all of that later, as we grow and want to explore other options and technology.

Initially, we are only planning eBooks, with annual, Omnibus editions in print. Based on participation and success, we may go to individual print editions via one or more of the major POD players.

For you, the contributor, there is not going to be a check paid on publication. I understand that some writers will not wish to participate in such a publishing model. However, the royalty share means that you will continue to earn money on any issue for as long as we keep them in print, with more issues generating you more money as time goes.

Story specs are fairly traditional. 2,000 – 9,000 words, on the selected theme and within the realm of science fiction. I'm not doing a horror magazine, or western, or fantasy, although we will explore how to publish all three of those themes into a pure SF story at some point in future issues. Nothing erotica, as this needs to be "all ages appropriate" for the most sales. All artists will agree to grant the magazine a three-month, world-wide, English-language, exclusive right from initial publication, and a non-expiring, non-exclusive right of publication worldwide after that. Put in simple terms, you don't get to come back later and demand that I take the issue down, and I plan to have them up there for a long time making all of us money for as long as Bundlerabbit survives.

We are only accepting original work. Read that as "no reprints" although we may want to do a "Best of" edition at some later date, all involved parties willing.

I (Blaze Ward, Founder) already plan to write into every issue. If I can build up a large-enough group of you willing to put in at least two stories per year, I will have enough material to justify the overall effort and turn this into something big. In addition, someone will be invited to write an essay exploring the theme of each issue and why it is important enough to pursue. That essay will count as a share for payment, so a single author might have two (or more, with editorial tasks) shares, with a TBD percentage of the overall reserved for cover art and editors, who will not work for free.

Since this is royalty-share, you (the artist) will be expected to advertise the magazine for your own greedy purposes. More money in equals more money (and hopefully prestige) for you. I don't figure we'll ever make enough money individually to qualify this for your SFWA bones, but I'm not a SFWA member at present and do not foresee circumstances where that would change. YMMV

What you will get out of being in The Syndicate is a cool membership card, and an open invitation to contribute to any issue. While I will occasionally invite guest creatives to participate in a single issue, I am not going to accept unsolicited manuscripts from non-Syndicalists. Membership has a price, however, and that price is writing me two stories each year. That's it. If you want to write four, be my guest. I will. If life happens and you can only write one, we'll review membership every year and can adjust expectations accordingly.

The Themes

This is a science fiction magazine, as I detailed above. All stories will be written in a specific science fiction category selected ahead of time. If you want to do fantasy, or westerns, this is probably not your Syndicate. I have grouped a series of ideas into (so-far) four large categories, to help us plan and balance flavors, like any decent cook:

Distant Space. Grand SF on galactic scales. Most of your favorite television shows and movies in your lifetime. Not-necessarily-Earth.

Near Space. Science fiction expected to have a harder, more scientific edge, and generally to be Earth-centered. (Whatever that means...)

Time Travel. What is science fiction without a good time travel story, or, better yet, alternate worlds where a character might slide between realities without control? The characters will be from the future, or encounter it, however, so this isn't just a cheap excuse to write historical fantasy and drape it SF terms, although both Saberhagen and King did exactly that, and better than you or I can.

'Punk. Cyber. Diesel. Steam. Clockwork. Toga. Stone. Exploring

themes where a radical, technological innovation threatens to upset the entire world, generally at the hands of a band of plucky rebels challenging an over-arching authority. Where Science Meets Fiction.

Year One

To make sure we have a good splash, I plan to pull a fast one on the readership. We will have the first four issues in the can and ready to drop before we make any public moves, while working on Issue #5. At that point, I will publish #1 quietly, followed roughly two weeks later by Issue #2. Roughly two weeks after that, I will publish Issue #3 and put a major advertising push behind it, along with a "did you know we already have several issues out?" all innocent and stuff.

The hope is that #3 is big, and entices people to go back and pick up #1 and #2, as completists tend to do. From the day we drop #3, the clock will start counting, with #4 coming out three months later.

To stay on my own, personal Amazon pulse, I plan to drop them on or about the 8th of each target month, so I can claim them on the 10th and get Amazon to send out a notice to all my fans that I have a new title out.

Starting with #3, I hope we will all start an advertising cycle designed to draw in readers. Because there will be three issues available at that point, I'm hoping there is a pretty big pool of Syndicate members interested in driving our readership, especially with #4 coming out on a fixed date.

The Mission Statement

As we were planning this project, someone muttered the infamous phrase that has become our corporate mission: "On theme. With weird."

I want margins pushed. Comfort zones violated. Rails ignored. Axes ground: political, sociological, economic, racial. I've already proved my point by previously editing "the adventures of Klan-man" in an anthology at the same time I wrote a Dystopian, Post-Trump-Apocalyptic Cowboy series, so I'm not generally going to be offended, as long as you don't turn into a troll and annoy the hell out of me or anybody else in the Syndicate, which will get your ass bounced quickly. Controversy will generate conversations, as well as sell issues. Keep that in mind.

Go weird or go home. Questions?

Issue List

Year One

- **Captain's Log ("Winter 2018")**
- *For many of us, those opening words "Captain's Log…" were our introduction to our science fiction dreams. Voyages to explore strange, new worlds, seek out new life, and boldly go. What will we find out there, when we go? What dangers will we confront? Who will survive?*
- Essay: "Who are we? Why are we doing this?" (Blaze)
- **Tuesday After Next ("Spring 2018")**
- *Not all science fiction is about galactic exploration. Right now, the future is being born as computers grow ever-more-powerful, and technology wrests control of the industrial heights from the traditional powers. After Dieselpunk and before Cyberpunk, you have the Makers and the Hackers, modern rebels hiding and striking from the shadows. Welcome to the Tuesday After Next.*
- Makerpunk/Hackerpunk
- Essay: The state of the art (Joel?)
- **Grand Theft Starship ("Summer 2018")**
- *The future is not always a bright and shining beacon on a hill somewhere. Crime will follow us into space and the galaxy. What will you steal, with the whole galaxy to pick from?*
- Something "big" stolen
- Essay: Why the fascination with crime?
- **Robots, Androids, Cyborgs, Oh My… (Fall 2018)**
- *We can make him better than he was. Or build a better one to replace him. What does it mean to be Sentient? Human? Or even alive?*

- "challenge Planet Bob to come up with something *different*"
- Essay: When does the Turing Test convey citizenship?

Year Two

- **Boneyard of Lost Dreams (Winter 2019)**
- *All spaceships, like all travelers, grow old and retire someplace quiet, until someone comes along. What will you find on the old derelict? Or hiding in the junkyard of forgotten starships and lost dreams?*
- figure that someone will go horror
- also the child who finds a prize
- Essay: Recycling History
- **Ray Guns and Space Babes (Spring 2019)**
- *Pulp. Freshly squeezed. Throw it back to bad 30's and 40's tropes and archetypes. Lantern-jawed heroes. Femme fatales .Scantily-clad princesses. Scenery chewing villains. And Dr. Basil Exposition in a white coat.*
- Silly, satirical, over the top pulp
- Essay: Tropes
- **Apocalypse Descending (Summer 2019)**
- *The world is ending. Right here. Right now. How? Why? What's next?*
- Stories about a world about to end, in the process, or picking up the pieces the next morning.
- Essay: (?)
- **Comet Wranglers And Asteroid Miners (Fall 2019)**
- *So it turns out Einstein was right. FTL is not possible and we are pretty much stuck here. What happens to humanity when the stars turn out to be unreachable dreams?*
- Hard SF in the home solar system
- Essay: Orbital physics and hand-waving.

Year Three

- **Alien Dreams (Winter 2020)**
- *What is science fiction, if not an exploration of who we'll find*

when we get out there? What will they be like? Alien life. Alien viewpoints. Alien Dreams.

- No humans allowed (as heroes)
- Essay: (?)
- **Homo Futuris (Spring 2020)**
- *Medicine is on the verge of conquering disease and aging. Of making it possible to clone ourselves and make our children super beings. Or morlocks. What will the world be like when science conquers life itself?*
- Clones and mad scientist issues.
- Essay: Ethics and definitions of being human (?)
- **What Might Have Been (Summer 2020)**
- *Time travel stories are as old as science fiction, wandering backwards to change the past or forward like Buck Rogers trapped in that abandoned mine shaft. Perhaps you will step through a mirror darkly. How will the world change? How will you?*
- Time Travel/Alternate Worlds issue
- Essay: (Bruno?)
- **Lawmen and Crimefighters (Fall 2020)**
- *Crime will go into space faster than law enforcement jurisdictions. What will the wild west of deep space look like, to the men and women who have to protect it?*
- Flip side of Grand Theft issue
- Focus on the badge or the PI
- Essay: (?)

Themes List

Distant Space (Grand SF)

- The terraforming work crew
- Josh: "How I Would Have Done It."
- Avast! (The Pirate Issue)
- The Captain's Log
- Alien Viewpoints
- Cargo wars

- End of Empires
- Music of the Spheres
- Space Barbarians
- Dark matter
- Intergalactic plasma space dragons
- Space wrecks - Lost Dreams - The Boneyard
- Ray Guns And Space Babes
- Lawmen
- Transluminal
- Desert Worlds
- Pioneers
- Grand Theft Starship
- Lost civilizations
- Glitter Guns/choose your weapon (The Armaments Issue)
- The Cosmic Ballet
- Ascended
- Space Fantasy
- Wandering Monsters – horror issue
- Darkly Beautiful

Near Space (Hard SF)

- Invasion
- Cold Equations - thuringwell
- Stowaways
- "Robots, and Androids, and Cyborgs, Oh My"
- Robot sidekicks
- Uncanny Valley
- Hacking her smart bra
- Comet wildcatters and asteroid miners
- Breaking the laws of physics
- Clones and artificial life forms, supermen
- Eclipsed
- Dancing the solar winds
- The Psychic Deli
- Hang-gliding on mars

Time Travel

- Alternate worlds
- Sliders
- Strangers in Strange lands

'Punk

- Tuesday After Next
- Punk, Cyber Punk
- Mad Science
- Steam/Diesel/Toga-punk/Weird West steampunk
- Post apocalypse
- Roadtrip back from the end of the world

The Syndicate Notes

Issue Specifications

- Payment will be a royalty share with a fixed percentage (TBD) assigned to the editorial team and the remainder evenly split among all stories.
- A single story with multiple authors still counts as a single share.
- Multiple stories by a single author will count for multiple shares.
- We will start with eBook and reserve the right to do paper if possible.
- Paper issues may contain external ("not any of the authors") advertising at the discretion of the Executive. We will refrain from political ads whenever possible.

- Back matter will be a one-paragraph bio and single image (TBD) for each contributor.
- Our goal is to do an annual Omnibus that contains all four issues, perhaps with supplementary materials.

Syndicate Membership rules

- Modify a copy of the UA membership agreement
- Syndicalist will sign (one-time) an agreement detailing Syndicate membership
- Syndicalist will agree to participate in each collaboration/issue they submit stories for by a certain, up-front deadline
- Syndicalist User will maintain an account in good standing on Bundlerabbit.com
- Syndicalist will maintain an active paypal account (BR will handle all the money)
- Syndicalist will commit to being in at least two issues (life rolls notwithstanding) with membership reviewed annually by the Executive.
- Syndicalist agrees to allow sales and specials on all issues they participate in.
- This may include bundling issue and print omnibus editions.
- Syndicalist agrees to provide accurate and up-to-date bio and cv information for website and back-matter pages.
- Syndicalists can suggest future themes to the Executive.

Guest Creatives rules

- Guest will agree to participate in each collaboration/issue they submit stories for
- Guest will maintain an account in good standing on Bundlerabbit.com

- Guest will maintain an active paypal account (BR will handle all the money)
- Guest agrees to allow sales and specials on their issue.
- This may include bundling the issue and print omnibus editions.

BundleRabbit Collaboration

1. Create a collaboration (Issue #1)
2. Invite participants
3. Edit each participant's percentage
4. Include fixed fee for Editorial tasks. 30%?
5. Lock the participants
6. Each participant must agree to the BR contract.
7. One-time Syndicate contract
8. Setup the eBook prices for each currency.
9. Rules for length or fixed?
10. Set up each sales channel (enter the meta data, upload cover & content)
11. Publish on each sales channel.

19

APPENDIX TWO: THE SYNDICATE CONTRACT

Following is the contract as I put it to the original group of Syndicate members. Pros who I know and respect looked at this and used it to recruit a couple of other people for me, because they thought it was such a writer-friendly gig. And I agree, as both Editor and Syndicate writer.

Memorandum Of Agreement

This contract is made between Knotted Road Press, Inc., hereinafter referred to as the PUBLISHER, and_____, hereinafter referred to as the AUTHOR.

Recitals

1. Boundary Shock intends to be a quarterly science fiction magazine published by Publisher through its chosen distributor (presently to be the mechanism of Bundle Rabbit (www.bundlerabbit.com)), hereinafter referred to as the DISTRIBUTOR

2. Participant is a writer who has agreed to join a Syndicate of writers for the purpose of providing a reliable, ongoing source of science fiction stories and essays for Boundary Shock.

3. Membership in the Syndicate grants the author the right to

contribute a story or an invited essay, hereinafter the WORK, into any issue of Boundary Shock, with an expectation that they will contribute at least two Works per calendar year.

4. Membership in the Syndicate will be regularly reviewed at the publisher's sole discretion for ongoing participation and recruiting new authors, as needed.

5. Publisher will occasionally invite Guest Authors to participate, under a separate contract, for specific issues of Boundary Shock, on an individual basis.

Agreement

1. Author has agreed to regularly contribute to the Boundary Shock magazine. The minimum length of each participant's Work shall be 2,000 words, and not more than 9,000 words, with the overall length of author's Work to be at publisher's discretion. Visual artists may contribute ten full-page illustrations, or a ten-page graphic novel to be eligible for a full share. Short poetry works, smaller art submissions, and flash fiction under 2,000 words will be considered at publisher's sole discretion and offered a half share (see Payments below) if selected.

2. (a) Boundary Shock entails the following rights: First-publication World Ebook, Print, and Audio Rights.

(b) These rights are held exclusively for three (3) months after publication in Boundary Shock and non-exclusively as long as that particular edition of Boundary Shock remains available for purchase.

3. The Publisher retains the sole right to remove a Work from an issue at a later date and republish that issue of the magazine with that Work no longer included, as circumstances warrant. Payment shares would then be adjusted accordingly (See Payment below).

4. (a). The Author grants to the Publisher the nonexclusive, worldwide English-language right to republish the Work or cause the Work to be republished in any book or anthology consisting of material at least 50% of which originally appeared in Boundary Shock, and which includes works by three or more contributors.

(b) The Author grants to the Publisher the nonexclusive, worldwide right to translate and republish the Work or cause the

Work to be republished in any book or anthology consisting of material at least 50% of which originally appeared in Boundary Shock, and which includes works by three or more contributors.

(c) The Author grants to the Publisher the Non-Exclusive right to excerpt the Works in non-book printed materials, blogs, social media posts, and other mediums for the sole purpose of promoting the Works.

5. The Author grants Publisher the right to use the Author's name, image, likeness, and biographical material for any advertising, promotion and other exploitation of the Work. Upon request, the Author shall provide the Publisher with a photograph or acceptable likeness of the Author and appropriate biographical material for such use.

6. The Author warrants that he or she is the sole author of the Work; that he or she is the owner of all the rights granted to the Publisher hereunder and has full power to enter into this agreement and to make the grants herein contained; that the Work is original and any prior publication of the Work in whole or in part has been fully disclosed to the Publisher; that the Work does not violate the right of privacy of any person; that, to the author's knowledge, it is not libelous or obscene and contains no matter which is libelous, in violation of any right of privacy, harmful to the user or any third party so as to subject the Publisher to liability or otherwise contrary to law; and that it does not infringe upon any copyright or upon any other proprietary or personal right of any person, firm, or corporation.

7. The Author will indemnify the Publisher against any loss, injury, or damage finally sustained (including any legal costs or expenses and any compensation costs and disbursements paid by the Publisher) occasioned to the Publisher in connection with or in consequence of any breach of this warranty and which the Publisher is not able to recover under its insurance policies.

8. The Publisher will make no alterations to the Work's text or title without the Author's written approval in e-mail or hardcopy. The Publisher reserves the right to make minor copyediting changes to conform the style of the text to its customary form and usage.

9. If the Publisher fails to publish the Work within twelve (12) months of the date of the originally intended release date for a

particular issue, all rights granted hereunder shall immediately revert to the Author.

10. The Publisher agrees to list a proper copyright notice for the Work in the name of the Author on an appropriate copyright page.

11. The Author will be credited on the table of contents page and at the beginning of the Work.

12. All rights not expressly granted by the Author are reserved by the Author.

Payment And Distributor

1. Boundary Shock will be published via the Distributor as a collaboration, using Distributor's royalty-share payment system. There will be no up-front payment to the author for participation in any given issue.

2. The author will received a share of net profits (defined as gross receipts received from Distributor after they take their fees). This share equals 75% (seventy-five percent) of net divided by the number of Works in the issue for the right to use the Work in all original language print, e-book, and audio editions of the specific issue. If the issue contains Works receiving a half share, other shares will be adjusted accordingly.

3. Author will maintain an active account in good standing on the Distributor selected by the Publisher for purposes of participation in any given issue of Boundary Shock and payment of royalties.

4. Payment will use the royalty-share method on Distributor's system, with Distributor being solely responsible for accurate and timely payments of all royalties to all participants, rather than the Publisher. The Distributor will split the net profits evenly for each issue based on the rotating cast of authors who participated in any given issue.

Execution

Regardless of its place of execution, this agreement shall be interpreted under the laws of the State of Washington, USA.

The parties acknowledge that each party has read and understood this contract before execution.

Author

Date

Publisher

Date

READ MORE!

Be sure to pick up the other books in the Business for Breakfast series!

The Beginning Professional Writer
The Beginning Professional Publisher
The Beginning Professional Storyteller
The Intermediate Professional Storyteller
Business Planning for Professional Publishers
The Healthier Professional Writer
The Three Act Structure for Professional Writers
How to Launch a Magazine for Professional Publishers
Pulp Speed for the Professional Writer
Growing as a Professional Artist

ABOUT THE AUTHOR

Blaze Ward writes science fiction in the Alexandria Station universe (Jessica Keller, The Science Officer, The Story Road, etc.) as well as several other science fiction universes, such as Star Dragon, the Collective, and more. He also writes odd bits of high fantasy with swords and orcs. In addition, he is the Editor and Publisher of *Boundary Shock Quarterly Magazine*. You can find out more at his website www.blazeward.com, as well as Facebook, Goodreads, and other places.

Blaze's works are available as ebooks, paper, and audio, and can be found at a variety of online vendors (Kobo, Amazon, and others). His newsletter comes out quarterly, and you can also follow his blog on his website. He really enjoys interacting with fans, and looks forward to any and all questions—even ones about his books!

Never miss a release!
If you'd like to be notified of new releases, sign up for my newsletter.

I will never spam you or use your email for nefarious purposes. You can also unsubscribe at any time.

http://www.blazeward.com/newsletter/

Connect with Blaze!

Web: www.blazeward.com
Boundary Shock Quarterly (BSQ):
https://www.boundaryshockquarterly.com/

ABOUT KNOTTED ROAD PRESS

Knotted Road Press fiction specializes in dynamic writing set in mysterious, exotic locations.

Knotted Road Press non-fiction publishes autobiographies, business books, cookbooks, and how-to books with unique voices.

Knotted Road Press creates DRM-free ebooks as well as high-quality print books for readers around the world.

With authors in a variety of genres including literary, poetry, mystery, fantasy, and science fiction, Knotted Road Press has something for everyone.

Knotted Road Press
www.KnottedRoadPress.com